The Patriotic Gu

22 Patriotic Guitar Solos for Fingerpickers a

Arranged by Larry McCabe

"Stand with anybody that stands right. Stand with him while he is right, and part from him when he goes wrong."

A. LINCOLN.

Credits

Cover Photographs by Ann Dickinson Photography, Tallahassee, Florida.
Arranger and guitarist: Larry McCabe
Engineer: Perry Nelson
Inspiration: George Washington, Thomas Jefferson, Thomas Paine,
William Billings, Abraham Lincoln, Julia Ward Howe,
John Philip Sousa, and American patriots and veterans in every era.

Special thanks to Andy Robinson at Taylor Guitars

ISBN 1-57424-117-6
SAN 683-8022

About the Author

Originally from Kansas City, Missouri, Larry McCabe received an education degree from the University of Arizona in 1979. Since then, he has worked as a freelance music teacher, teaching more than 30,000 private music lessons as well as classes on American music history. Besides teaching, Larry has written over forty music books on a wide range of subjects including songwriting, guitar, banjo, fiddle, and electric bass.

A member of the nominating committee for the annual W.C. Handy Blues Awards, Larry has shared his blues guitar expertise in columns for *Living Blues* magazine and *Fingerstyle Guitar* magazine. His former teacher, the late Eldon Shamblin, was the rhythm guitarist and arranger for Bob Wills – the "King of Western Swing" – for many years.

As coordinator of the McCabe WWII History Project, Larry has collected hundreds of stories about senior American's experiences during the tumultuous Depression and World War II years. The first oral history book of McCabe Project stories, *We Remember Pearl Harbor* is almost complete. A second book will feature stories about WWII experiences, told by those who served out nation in uniform and on the home front.

Another of Larry's interests is folk fiddling. He currently lives in Tallahassee, Florida with his wife Becky, who along with Larry is a member of the Blue Bayou Cajun Band.

Information about private music lessons with Larry McCabe can be found at mccabemusic.com.

This book is dedicated to the memory
of my dad and all his WWII comrades

Book Description ---~

The Patriotic Guitarist features 22 traditional patriotic songs arranged for intermediate fingerstyle and flatpicking guitar. All the songs – many of which have never before been available in print for solo guitar – are suitable for solo performance. Historical/anecdotal notes and composer's names are included with each song. The book is accompanied by a CD, which includes note-for-note solo acoustic guitar performances of every song. As you play these songs, you will be educating as well as entertaining others while helping to perpetuate our heritage of freedom.

Songs: America; America the Beautiful; Assembly; Battle Hymn of the Republic; The Caisson Song; Chester; Dixie; Garry Owen; The Girl I Left Behind Me; Green Grow the Lilacs; Home! Sweet Home!; It's a Long Way to Tipperary; Jefferson and Liberty; Johnny Has Gone for a Soldier; Liberty/The Eighth of January medley; The Marines' Hymn; O, Canada; The Star Spangled Banner; Taps; When Johnny Comes Marching Home; Yankee Doodle; You're a Grand Old Flag.

CD Description ---~

The Patriotic Guitarist CD features solo guitar performances of all songs in the book of the same title – 22 songs in all. The songs are played in the "no frills, down home pickin' style" of author Larry McCabe. Most of the songs are played twice through to facilitate extended practice. The CD is great for listening, learning, and giving as a gift to anyone who loves good music. This is truly a unique, hard-to-find item.

Fingerings ---~

Recommended fingerings for the fretting hand appear in the notation staff. Feel free to change any fingerings as necessary to suit your own particular style.

1=First finger (index) 2=Second finger (middle)
3=Third finger (ring) 4=Little finger (pinky)

Folk and blues guitarists often use the thumb to fret the following chords: 1) Open-string D; 2) Open-string D7; 3) "F-shape" barre chords. The indication **"Th."** next to a bass note indicates that the note can be fretted with the thumb, especially on steel-string guitars.

In most cases, picking-hand fingerings are omitted. Because classical guitarists use a different approach than folk and blues guitarists, picking-hand fingerings are left to the discretion of the performer.

Table of Contents

3rd U.S. Infantry Band, Jefferson Barracks, Missouri, 1867. The instrumentation of this Regular Army band includes one trombone and a variety of upright, OTS, and bell front horns. The valve instruments have either Berliner piston or American string rotary valves. The snare drummer is using a rod tension side drum. Rod tension drums are rarely seen in early band photographs.

1916

America

First sung in Park Street Church, Boston, July 4, 1832.

Words by Samuel Francis Smith (1808-1895)
Author of music unknown

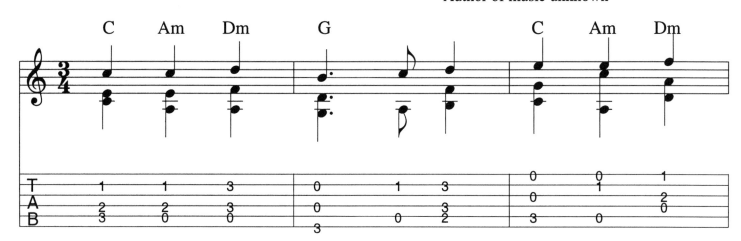

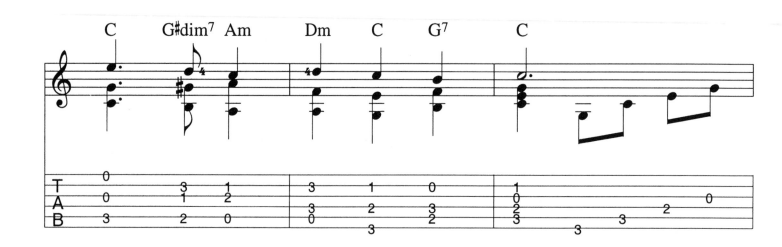

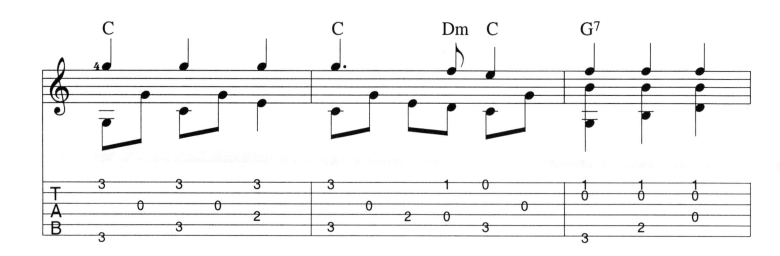

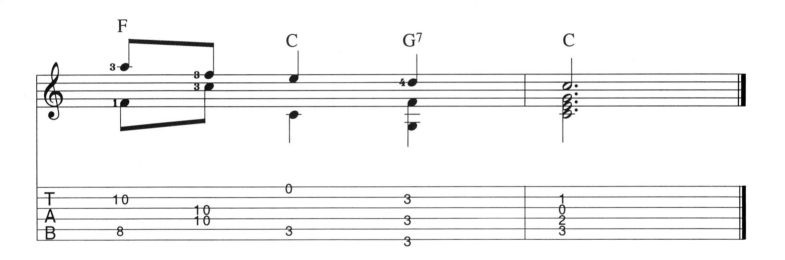

America the Beautiful

Katharine Lee Bates' poem, "American the Beautiful," was first printed on July 4, 1895. By 1910 someone–it is not known who–had set her words to Samuel A. Ward's 1882 composition, "Materna."

Music by Samuel Augustus Ward (1847-1903)
Words by Katherine Lee Bates (1859-1929)

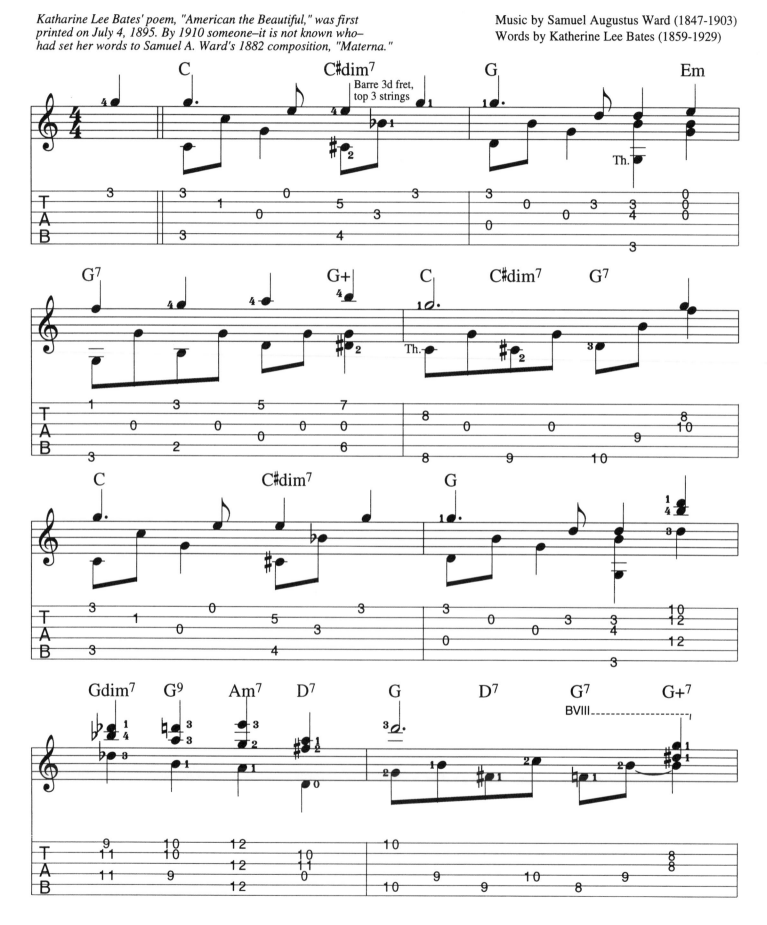

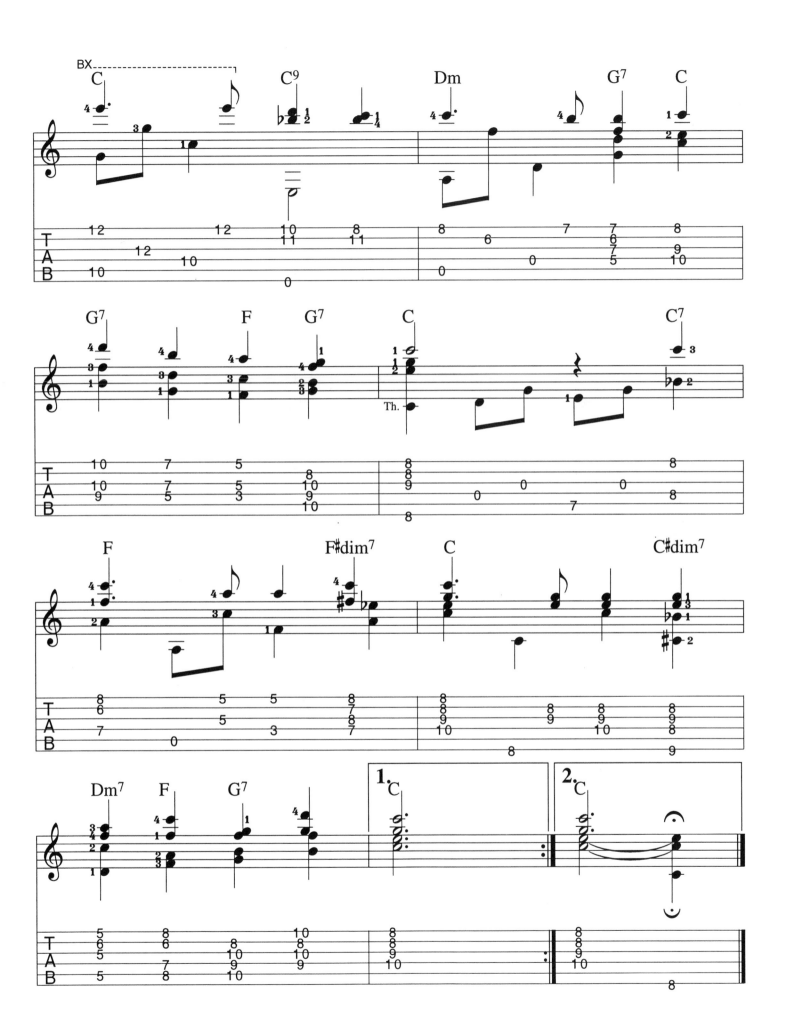

Assembly

This famous bugle call was first published in Savannah, Ga., in 1842.

American Bugle Call

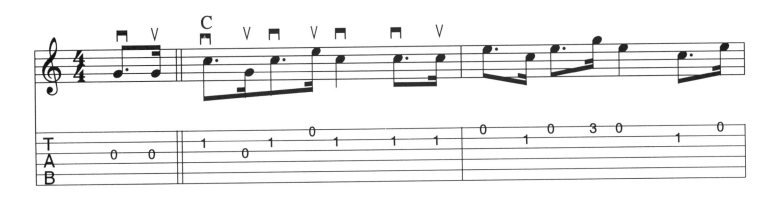

1918

Battle Hymn of the Republic

*Mrs. Howe, a remarkable, multi-talented woman, wrote this
stirring poem after visiting Union encampments with her
likewise accomplished husband, Dr. Samuel G. Howe, in 1861.*

Words by Julia Ward Howe (1819-1910)
Author of music unknown

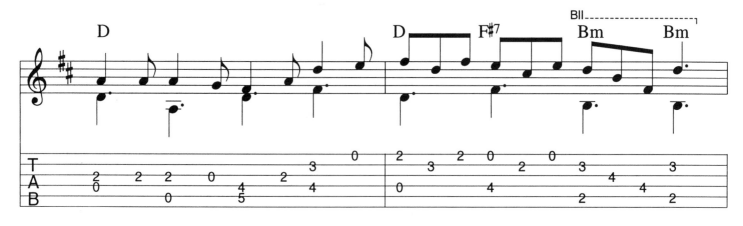

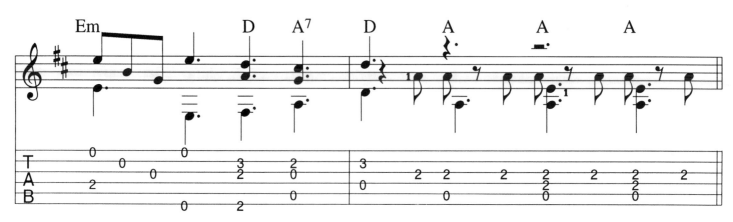

14

TRACK 6

Caisson Song

(The Caissons Go Rolling Along)

Edmund L. Gruber, a 1904 graduate of West Point and career Army man, wrote "The Caisson Song" for a 5th Artillery company reunion that was held in the Philippine Islands in 1907. John Philip Sousa's 1918 arrangement helped to popularize the song.

Edmund L. Gruber (1879-1941)

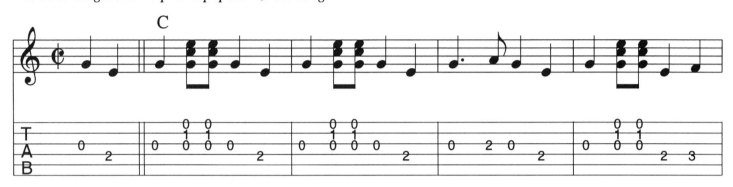

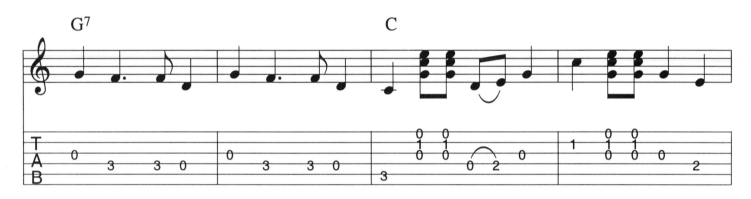

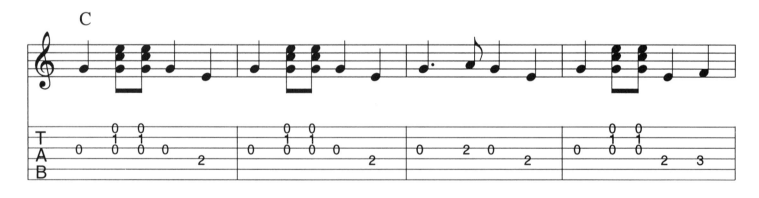

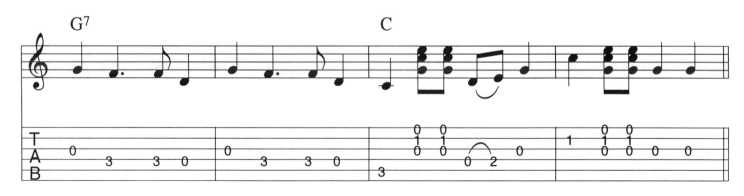

Chester

"Chester" has been called America's first great war song. The song's self-taught composer, William Billings of Boston, was a tanner by trade. His <u>New England Psalm-Singer</u> (1770) was the first published collection of American music.

William Billings (1746-1800)

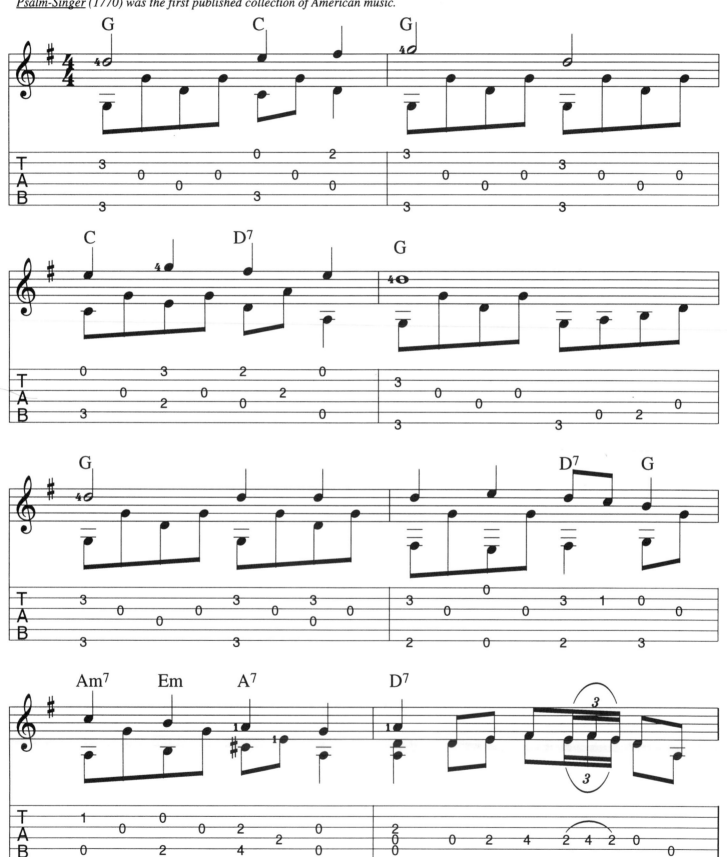

18

Dixie

Daniel Decatur Emmett (1815-1904)

"Dixie" was composed as a minstrel "walk-around" by Ohio native and minstrel musician "Jolly" Dan Emmett in 1859. Much to Emmett's chagrin, his creation soon became the unofficial anthem of the Confederacy. Emmett, a notable banjo picker in his day, also authored "Old Dan Tucker."

For best results, emphasize the melody notes in "Dixie" while playing the arpeggio notes and passing tones with a lighter touch. Be sure to alternate pick (down-up) each pair of eighth notes. A heavy flatpick is best for playing in this style.

Garry Owen

Traditional Irish

The lively Irish tune "Garry Owen" (or "Garryowen") has been popular with fifers, military bands, and marching soldiers ever since the Revolutionary War era. During the Civil War, this great jig was a favorite of both Union and Confederate troops, and it is said that Union Gen. George A. Custer ((1839-1876) was particularly fond of the tune. Some historians believe that "Garry Owen" may have been played for Custer as he marched off to meet Crazy Horse (1843?-1877) at the Little Bighorn in June 1876.

Custer's theme song is, of course, traditionally played at a marching tempo. The arrangement given here is played at a moderate speed. For an uptempo, "Custerized" version of "Garry Owen" pick only the melody notes, with a heavy flatpick.

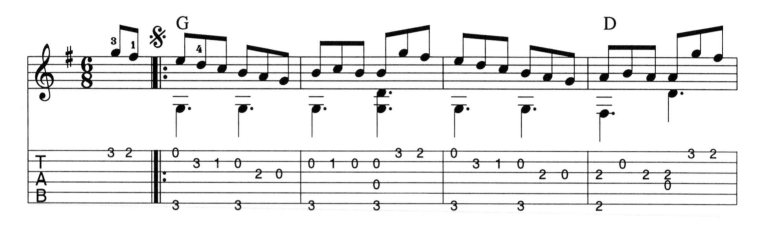

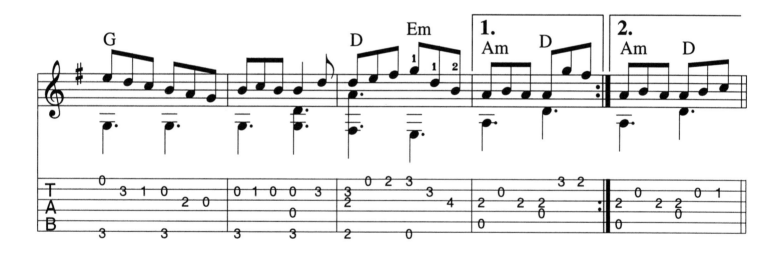

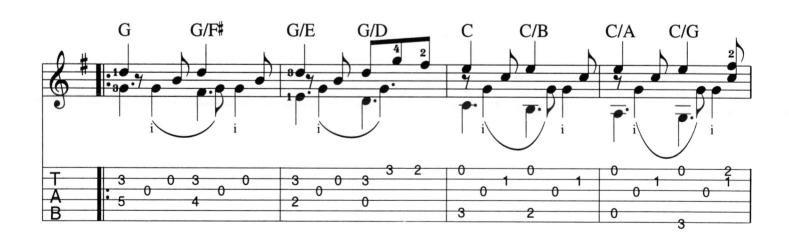

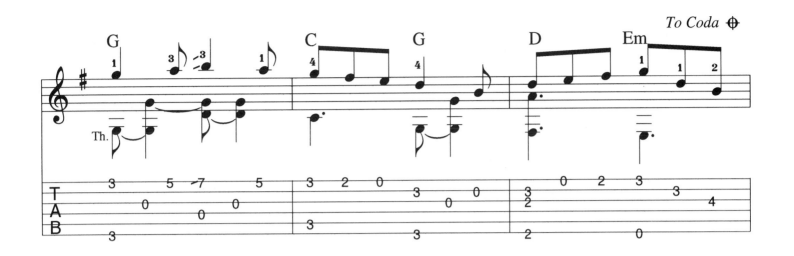

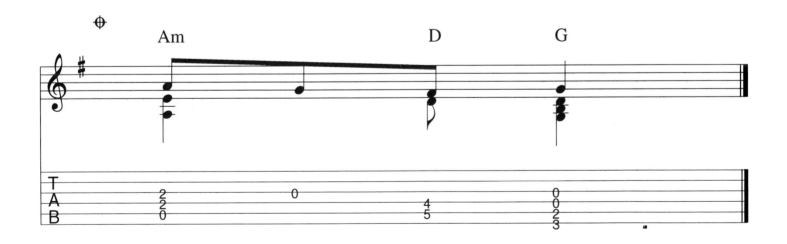

TRACK 10

The Girl I Left Behind

Traditional British

The melody for the enduring "The Girl I Left Behind Me" first appeared in print around 1810. In 1818 the Irish poet Thomas Moore reworked the melody into its present form, for a song that appeared in his "A Selection of Irish Melodies." The (normally) jaunty tune is fingerpicked here at a slow, "Lord, I wanna go home" tempo. Skip the bass notes, and flatpick the melody, if you want to speed things up.

Green Grow the Lilacs

Anonymous

"Green Grow the Lilacs" dates back to the Mexican-American War (1846-1848). At that time, Americans were introduced to the term "gringo" by the song's original title, "Gringo the Lilacs." Who wrote this lovely, timeless ballad? We simply do not know.

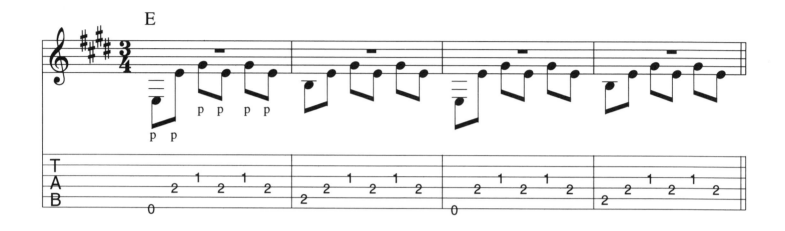

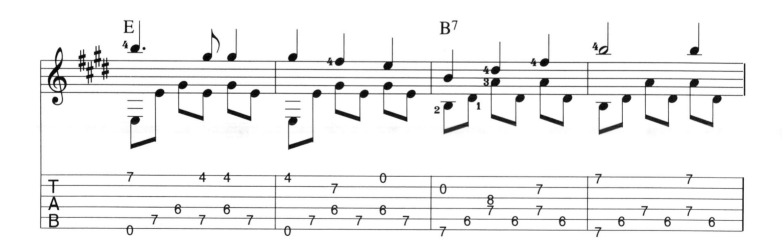

26

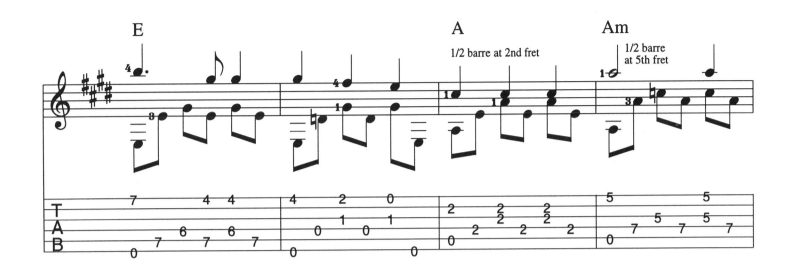

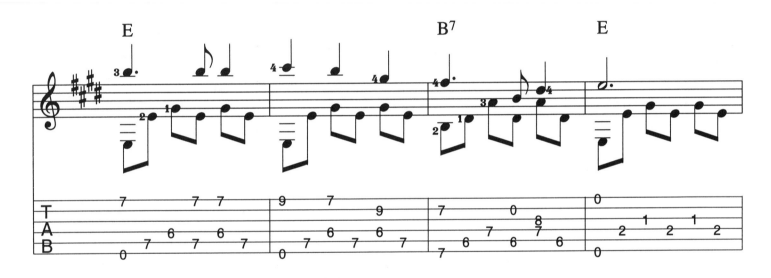

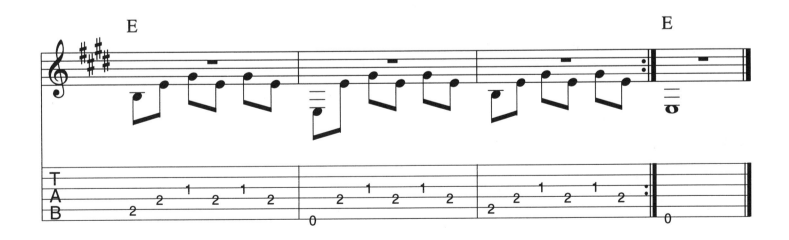

Home! Sweet Home!

Payne, a lifelong wanderer, wrote the words in 1923; his poem was then set to Bishop's 1821 melody (which had originally accompanied other lyrics). This is perhaps the most famous "home is where the heart is" song of all time.

Music by Henry R. Bishop (1786-1855)
Lyrics by John Howard Payne (1791-1852)

It's a Long Way to Tipperary

This rollicking 1912 British vaudeville song became very popular during WWI, first with British tommies, then with American dougboys. County Tipperary is in the S. central Republic of Ireland; the county town is also named Tipperary.

Jack Judge (1878-1938)
Harry Williams (1874-1924)

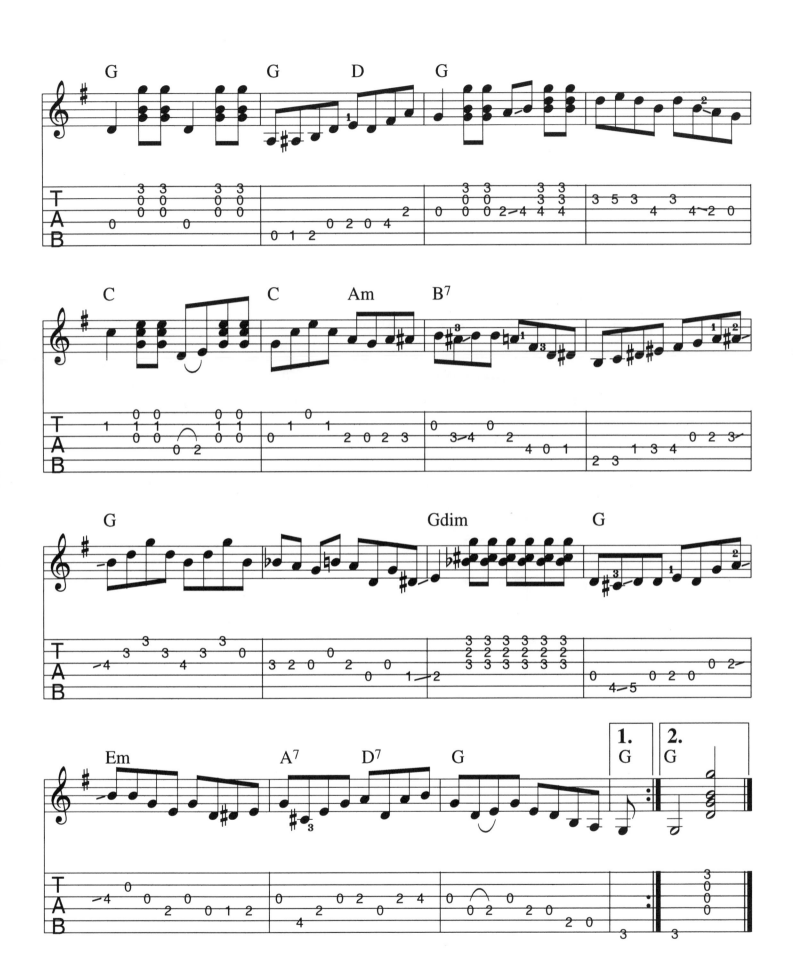

Jefferson and Liberty

Thomas Jefferson's campaign song of 1804, with lyrics by John Treat Paine set to the Irish jig, "The Gobby-O." The tune, which has also been called "Paul Revere's Ride," has long been a standard among fifers; it was played by both Union and Confederate bands during the Civil War. "Gob-stick" was a slang term for a fife. Played in the dorian mode.

Traditional Irish Jig

Johnny Has Gone for a Soldier

Irish Air

A sad Irish air with lyrics that relate the suffering of a woman whose man has gone to war.
Popular in the U.S. during the French and Indian War, the American Revolution, and the
Civil War. Recently revived by Mark O'Connor and James Taylor for a PBS history program.

The melody is presented here in four variations.

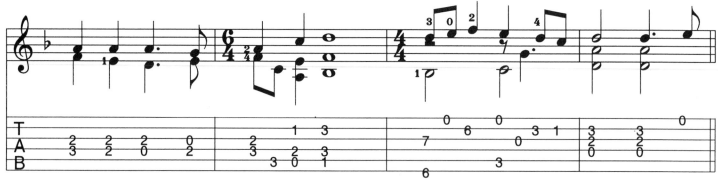

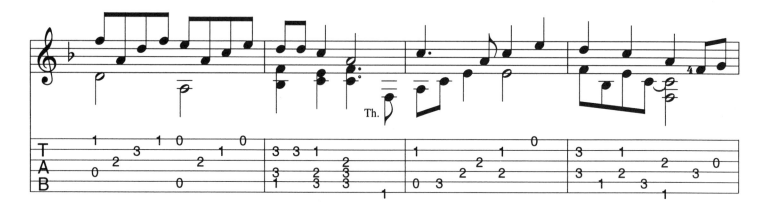

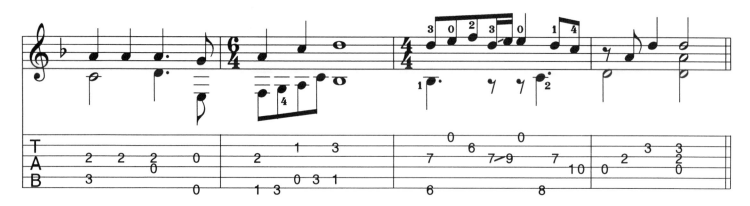

TRACK 16

Liberty

Traditional

Both of these fine old tunes–"Liberty" and "The Eighth of January"–seem to be red-blooded American creations (if perhaps derivative). "Liberty" is sometimes called "Reel de Ti-Jean" or "Tipsy Parson"; the former alternate title might indicate a French-Canadian influence.

"The Eighth of January" celebrates Gen. Andrew Jackson's (1767-1845) repulse of the British at the Battle of New Orleans, Jan. 8, 1815. The first part of an old tune entitled "Chase the Squirrel" bears some similarity to the first section of "Eighth of January." Likewise, the A section of the English morris dance tune, "Shepherds' Hey" resembles Old Hickory's commemorative tune.

The Eighth of January

TRACK 16 (second song of medley)

Two variations of this AB tune are presented here.

Traditional

TRACK 17

The Marines' Hymn

French composer Offenbach wrote the "Marines' Hymn" melody for a song in a French opera ca. 1868. Despite claims by several candidates, the lyricist for "The Marines' Hymn" remains unidentified. The first known appearance in print of words with music was in New York in 1918. Offenbach also wrote "Apache Dance."

Music by Jacques Offenbach (1819-1860)

Barre strings 2, 3, 4 at 2nd fret

TRACK 18

O, Canada

The original version of "O, Canada" (Lavallée-Routhier) was first sung publicly on St.–John Baptiste Day in 1880. In 1908, Robert S. Weir translated the lyrics into English. "O, Canada" was officially pronounced the Canadian national anthem in 1980.

Music by Calixa Lavallée (1842-1891)
French Lyrics by Sir Adolphe-Basile Routhier (1839-1920)
Official English Lyrics by Hon. Robt. Stanley Weir (1856-1926)

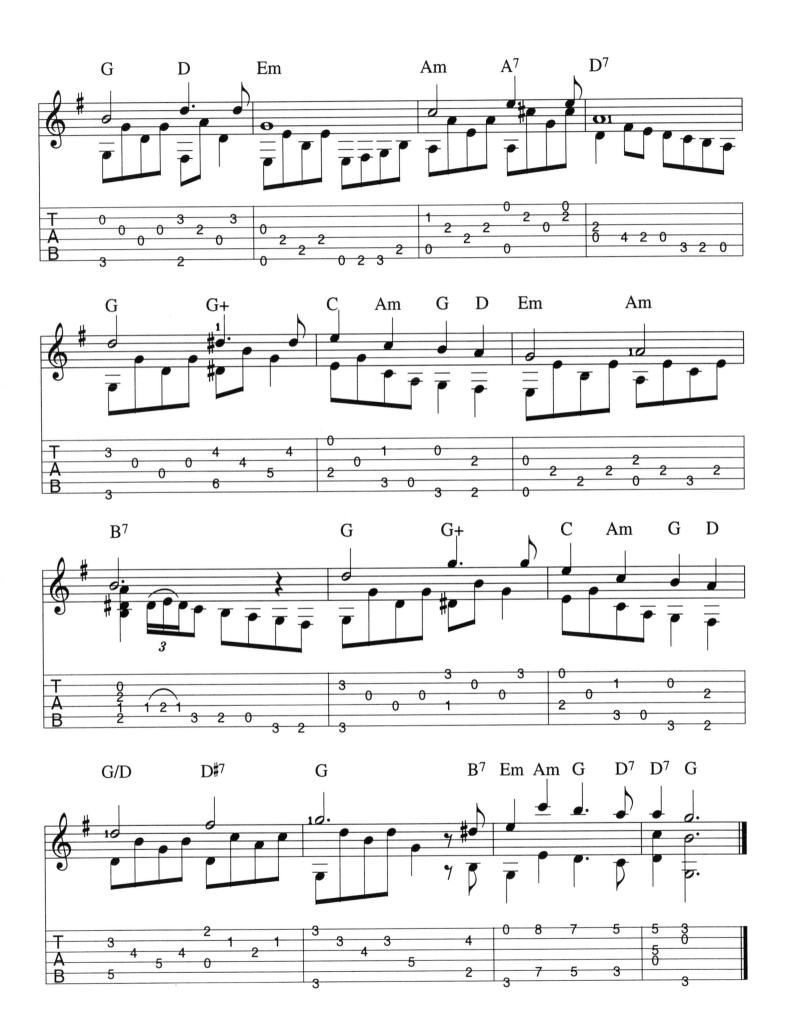

The Star Spangled Banner

Baltimore lawyer Key wrote the "Star Spangled Banner" poem as he witnessed the British bombardment of Fort McHenry on Sept. 13-14, 1814. The lyrics were set to the tune of "The Anacreontic Song," written by the English composer John S. Smith ca. 1777. In 1931 "The Star Spangled Banner" was declared the U.S. national anthem by an act of Congress.

Music by John Stafford Smith (1750-1836)
Words by Francis Scott Key (1780-1843)

Taps

Gen. Daniel Butterfield (1831-1901)

"Taps" was composed by General Butterfield in July 1862 while he was commanding a Union brigade on the James River in Virginia.

The renowned bugle call soon supplanted "To Extinguish Lights," the last call played at the end of the day in the Union Army. "Extinguish Lights" signaled that the soldiers were to cease activities for the day and put out all lights.

Before the Civil War ended, buglers began playing "Taps" at soldier's funerals; the tune is now best known as the soldier's farewell. The soothing melody has an especially powerful effect on those who recall friends and loved ones who sacrificed their lives for their country.

General Butterfield's immortal melody is an outstanding example of what musicians call "economy of statement." It is not known when, or why, the tune came to be known as "Taps."

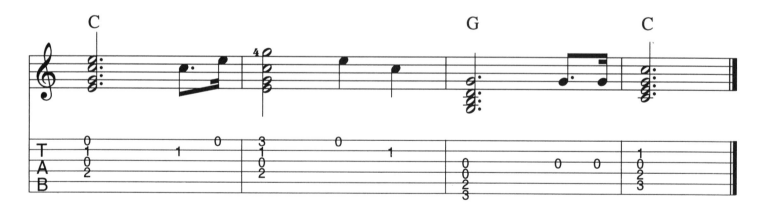

1912

When Johnny Comes Marching Home

TRACK 21

This unforgettable song was "introduced and performed by Gilmore's band" in 1863. Patrick S. Gilmore, a famous 19th-century bandmaster, was born in Ireland, came to Boston in 1847 and served in the Federal Army during the Civil War.

Patrick S. Gilmore (1829-1892)

Yankee Doodle

Our first national song, "Yankee Doodle" was long thought to be British in origin; many music historians now consider it to be a product of colonial America. This enduring ditty reflects both the humorous and patriotic elements of the national spirit.

Song of Colonial America

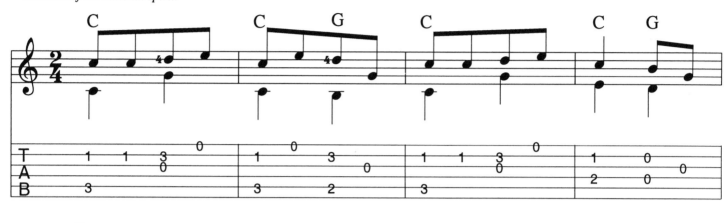

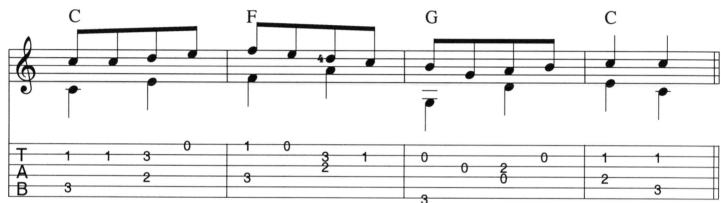

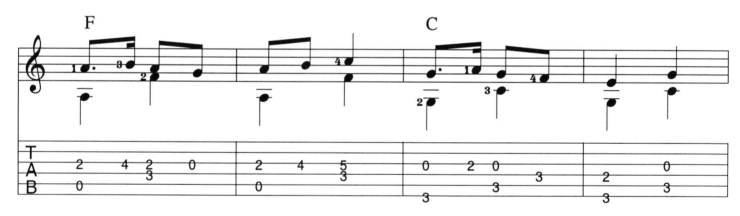

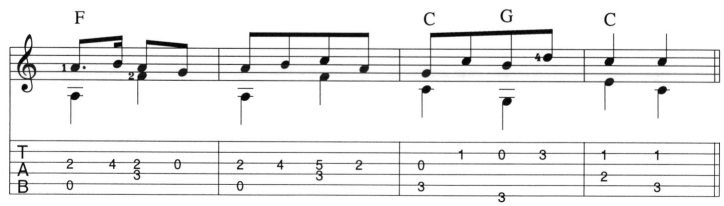

48

TRACK 23

You're a Grand Old Flag

One of Cohan's many American music masterpieces, "You're a Grand Old Flag" was written in 1906 for the musical show George Washington Jr. The song's original title, "You're a Grand Old Rag," was quickly modified following vigorous protests by patriotic organizations.

George M. Cohan (1878-1942)

50

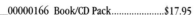